Affiliate Marketing Success Strategies

Toby Alexander

Copyright © 2022
All Rights Reserved

Table of content

Introduction

Chapter 1

The Top Reasons Why Beginners Should Use Affiliate Marketing to Earn Money

Chapter 2

Finding and Promoting Affiliate Products

Chapter 3

Making Smart Affiliate Product Selections

Chapter 4

Developing a Market and Promoting the Products

Chapter 5

Powerful Modern Tools and Strategies

Introduction

Part progressing is one of the most amazing ways for anybody to get cash on the web. This is a speedy and inactive technique to get essentially adaptable cash, and that is not difficult to set up. No specific dominance is required and on the off chance that you pick the right product and association point with the right market, you can make incalculable dollars in a short space of time.

Anyway we should keep up momentarily. Firstly what definitively is branch-off showing? How should it function? Furthermore what sorts out everyone of the subtleties essentially more amazing than other beneficial techniques for web business visionaries.

Branch-off propelling construes selling a product that isn't yours for a prize. You then need to get cash for every game plan you make proposing that all you genuinely ought to do is to interface that thing with a social occasion that will see the value in it.

While selling product for example eBooks you will constantly find that you get to keep 70% or a more critical proportion of the benefit! Pick the proper thing and you can get a comparable proportion of cash as somebody who constructed a product themselves.

In this book, you will become familiar with the advantages of part publicizing as well as how to set began rapidly and competently up to start gaining cash. With unbelievable thing choices, a coordinated multitude, and simply a touching piece of ideal karma this could change you as an affiliate marketer.

For those that are right now selling a product this book ought to give you the extra limits and tips you want to take your business to a more huge level genuinely. This coordinates the devices being involved by top brands to sell huge ticket things like MBA courses and $5,000+ durable workstations.

Chapter 1

The Top Reasons Why Beginners Should Use Affiliate Marketing to Earn Money

Associate progressing is an idea that evades various individuals. How would you get cash from selling something you didn't make?

How could it be that bringing genuine cash online can truly be immediate?

The most immediate strategy for making sense of it is that it is dealt with. You are going presumably as a trader and getting a commission on any game plans you make. In like that, you are like the house-to-house specialists who come around to sell your broadband.

What has an effect is that you're not going from house to house. The web is your entryway and this is an entry that gives you enlistment to everybody in the world. That speedily gives you an immense benefit and particularly when you figure out how you can get the guests to come to you.

The other separation here is that the commission plot will be essentially unique. Standard sales reps will ordinarily get to some degree cut of anything that they sell maybe

5-10%. As alluded to the separation with accessory displaying, is that you will get as much as 70-80% of the benefits. Believe it or not: a significant part of the time as helper support you are genuinely going to get more than the maker of the product.

This is the very thing that makes publicizing so hugely secure because it recommends that you can start getting corresponding like you were selling your own product, however without dealing with loads of cash to make something with no preparation.

Plus, is that since you'll sell a product that is as of now out there you can pick something that is by and by selling collectively. Right when you make your own product to sell, there is dependably a little wagered that you'll foster something that nobody necessities. Right when you just market something especially notable, that turns out to be broadly less possible.

One more enormous advantage of part displaying is the very way that adaptable it is. If you make a particular site page selling the benefits of something accessory, then, you can begin benefitting from it in no time flat. In that the case then, at that point, what is to hold you back from making one more page to sell something else? Also one more page to sell something else.

How Affiliate Marketing Works

Considering everything we should get somewhat more specific will we. How exactly does helper propelling capacity and how might a maker whenever be glad to offer such an unprecedented game plan for their benefits. As a matter of some importance might we at any point consider the kind of product you will sell. To different advertisers assistance product will be advanced product. There are more choices, which we will investigate in this book later. Anyway the product we'll zero on. That construes product like eBooks, online courses and introductions.

Motorized products are quickly a decent decision for selling on the web since they have zero overheads and no 'Machine gear pieces (this is a business term implying 'Cost Of Goods Sold'. That recommends that the maker doesn't need to pay out involving all possible means for every course of action and they can rather make gains and recommendations that benefit. It additionally proposes they never expected to deal with a lot of cash direct and they don't need to oversee transport no different either way. Hence, the maker no doubt made this modernized product themselves utilizing Word or a camera, or maybe they re-appropriated the creation to another person. Some way or another, they will have made this exceptional book not permanently set up to sell it for benefit.

Then at that point, the organizer will have started selling imparted things from their website page or an erratic page on the web. They'll try to drive whatever amount of traffic as could sensibly be anticipated to their site to request that individuals purchase from them and they'll have their automated sort of income.

In any case there's such an overflow of movement that one individual can do and in the end, their well will dissipate. That is where a maker could begin searching for branch-offs to work with to assist them with moving their product. What maker is subsequently prepared to offer assistance like us 70% or more since they need to assist us with selling their product. They comparatively need to urge us to sell their product instead of the product that different makers are offering accomplice projects for.

While the maker will at this point make 30% on their plans, this is as of now 30% more than they would have made on those courses of action in any case - because they could never have perhaps left.

Furthermore, on the off chance that that seller can draw in endless individuals to their books with a large number of online advertisers, they'll make titanic increments and in a general sense past what they could seclude.

This is a normally valuable strategy. The maker gets an additional 1,000 game plans by drawing in backers to work with them and helper get to sell a product like it were their own and maintain the greater part of the benefits! They can get a comparable proportion of pay as they would from their eBook or course, however without making one and facing that enormous test.

In particular, the way this cycle genuinely works is through the use of 'part affiliations' which subsequently work through treats.

Precisely when you find something associate you truly need to push, you will be given a section affiliation and this is the very thing you need to remember for your plans page and in your blog entries.

Precisely when a purchaser taps on your helper affiliation, they will at first be diverted to one more page on the web.

Here, a treat will be put away on their PC which will recollect them as having come from you. At this point, when they purchase something from that store, they will be recorded as being 'one of yours' and the award will be added to you all out for you to take out eventually. For you it's fundamental, advance the product and give the affiliation. It's just as simple as that.

Chapter 2

Finding and Promoting Affiliate Products

Alright, that is sufficient speculative talk, how would you get everything rolling and turned into a member advertiser? firstly you will require an item. To get this, you are going to need to make a beeline for a site like Clickbank or Commission Junction. Another great one is JVZoo.

Here, you'll have the option to see an enormous choice of various items that have partner programs. Simply look at and search for the ones you're keen on. You'll find that you can see some data in regards to the various items, so attempt to search for things that are selling at a respectable cost and proposition a decent commission.

A few destinations will allow you to see an unpleasant number of deals, in which case you need to search for the product which is selling great.

Whenever you've recognized the item you might want to advance, you then, at that point, need to contact the proprietor. Assuming you are effective, they'll give you your connection and you'll be allowed to involve that as you pick.

Another thing to remember here, however, is that many offshoot items will incorporate advertising materials alongside them.

Assuming you are getting along nicely, that implies that the maker is getting along nicely. They have a long list of motivations to need to see you succeed and in that capacity, they will give things like messages, a deals page, flag promotions, and different materials as a rule. On the off chance that you're new to the universe of showcasing, I enthusiastically suggest that you pick an item that offers these sorts of rewards. Along these lines, you can make it ready quickly by basically reordering the materials you have.

You ought to then see yourself sell in similar numbers it's a similar item and a similar showcasing routine so there's no great explanation that it shouldn't work comparably well. Like I said previously this is in a real sense a 'reorder' plan of action. Another person as of now has the item selling great with a set framework, all you are doing is duplicating a similar framework yet ensuring it's your ledger that will get the pay.

Selling Physical Products and Services

While selling eBooks through stages like JVZoo is a phenomenal method for guaranteeing that you can keep the most extreme benefit, it additionally has its restrictions. Despite everything that a few different advertisers could say to you, the most famous kind of item online is still the actual assortment.

What's more, this appears to be legit looking at the situation objectively. What number of individuals do you have any idea about who purchase actual items? Everybody right? However at that point what many individuals do you have any idea about who might purchase a digital book? Your Grandma could not (except if it's through Kindle) because she doesn't have any idea how to utilize a PDF record. Moreover, your companion who could do without perusing likely wouldn't by the same token. Furthermore, that fundamentally leaves you with a lot more modest cut of the market.

So how would we approach selling actual items as an offshoot advertiser? The most famous choice is to turn into an Amazon Associate.

Amazon's partner plot is their variant of a membership program and it's an exceptionally enticing choice for some advertisers. If you look into data on member showcasing, you'll probably find that by far most of it focuses on selling advanced items through any semblance of JVZoo, ClickBank and Commission Junction.

On Amazon the situation is unique. Amazon is as of now dividing the benefits with the producer, they need to pay for capacity, delivery, and postage, and by and large, they can't bear to offer you over 4% or perhaps 8% at a push. This implies you'll need to sell significantly more products at a lot greater costs to turn a legitimate benefit.

In any case, does that mean you ought to lead Amazon Associates out? Not in any way shape or form.

First off, selling actual items is in many cases considerably more beneficial than selling computerized items. Consider it, are you bound to burn through loads of cash on something you can grasp and show to companions, or something you need to peruse on a PC screen?

Amazon is a perceived brand and an organization individuals trust. That implies they're substantially more liable to purchase from them and they can purchase with a single tick.

Amazon has a gigantic list of items you can sell and that implies there will be a pertinent thing to go with essentially every article.

Lastly, assuming that somebody taps on your URL yet winds up purchasing something different from Amazon... you get compensated! This might bring about a ton of profit if somebody were to - for instance - purchase another PC and you were to get 8% of that. Regardless of whether you advance the item straightforwardly, as long as you sent the purchaser to Amazon in any case, you would procure that commission.

All in all the best thing to do? Utilize the two sorts of partner showcasing. Yet simply don't avoid Amazon with regards to the situation or you'll pass up a great opportunity.

In later sections you'll find how to advance Amazon items somewhat in an unexpected way to maximize them.

(Note: One restriction of Amazon Associates is that you can't bring in money on the off chance that you don't live in a similar country. All in all, if you are situated in the UK, you should send your clients to Amazon UK. You can in any case make deals through Amazon.com however, you'll simply have the option to gather vouchers in return.)

Different Options for Selling Physical Products

Amazon is not the most important platform in the world with regards to selling actual items. There are endless actual stores out there, as well as numerous makers that will offer member programs direct to advertisers.

You could view that as if you require some investment to search for different items, you're ready to find something considerably more straightforwardly pertinent to the subject of your site (and in this manner bound to sell).

To find these partner programs, simply take a stab at composing in your specialty and afterward "subsidiary program" while looking through on Google. You can likewise find a lot of records online for the best member programs in every industry.

Another choice is to coordinate a maker or merchant that doesn't offer a partner program… and afterward inquire as to whether they would consider making one for you. If you figure out how to do this effectively, you can hammer out a selective agreement and possibly get an enormous commission as well.

For everything to fall into place, you should have the option to show that you have the compass and the impact to make it worth your time and energy.

Selling Services

Another choice is to take a stab at selling a help or a SAS (Software As a Service). This choice is possibly the most rewarding.

The justification behind this is that many administrations will offer you a repetitive commission. Suppose that you figure out how to get somebody to join a betting site. Some betting destinations will offer a commission on all profit from that client for their lifetime with the brand.

Similarly, if you can persuade somebody to join with a facilitating account, or if not join a common help, then you will frequently observe that you are offered a commission that is paid to you each month that they stay with that facilitating organization.

This could begin as a modest quantity of commission. In any case, it can then amount to a lot of time. In a couple of years, you could have hundreds or even a huge number of transformations, which will then procure you repeating pay regardless of whether your site was to shut down.

Chapter 3

Making Smart Affiliate Product Selections

While partner publicizing is a marvelously clear and strong technique for getting cash on the web, it isn't thoroughly secure. As such that accepting you pick some unsatisfactory product, or market it erroneously, you likely won't see the brief kind of achievement you were anticipating.

A lot of your flourishing then will ride on your ability to pick the right thing. This is what you need to know.

What Not to Sell

By far most while picking a product to sell will pile up their auxiliary association of choice (ClickBank, JVZoo, WSOPro) and subsequently look for the product that have the most arrangements and the best commission.

This is a fair move since those figures suggest that others are getting a lot of money hence would it be smart for you to have the choice? You can from a genuine perspective 'reorder' their strategy honestly.

However, if that is all you're doing, you're committing a mistake. by far most of the product at the most elevated place of the posting will be a comparative precise product, getting cash electronically, dating or wellbeing.

If you start propelling one of those books, you're presently fighting with the large number of different people selling comparable books, and each one people selling tantamount books. A considerable number of individuals who have been involved on the web for more than a day are currently burnt out on being sold 'get cash from home undertakings'.

What's more, is that these are the most forceful claims to fame on the web. If you don't at this point have a massively successful website/mailing list, then, at that point, getting to the principal spot on Google for 'Acquire Money Online eBook' or 'Manufacture Muscle' will be close incomprehensible. You're setting yourself up in a way to miss the mark.

Elective Strategies

Maybe then, contemplate picking something in a more unassuming strength. Assume you find an eBook zeroed in on a specific industry or work - maybe something encouraging people on how to get cash from bloom coordinating. It has all the earmarks of being less astounding and the group is more unassuming yet your product is at present surprising.

What's more is that you can without a very remarkable stretch show up at those bloom arrangers by posting on several blossom web diaries. Besides, you can in all probability get your business page to the most noteworthy reason behind Google for 'sprout arranging eBook' essentially more easily. It has a sensible USP as well which makes it extraordinarily easy to sell.

Far superior nonetheless is to look at the courses to grandstand you at this point have. What contacts might you anytime at some point use? Why might you at anytime contact numerous people? What are those people propelled by?

Think about how you'll sell the thing and where you'll show up at your goal fragment before you pick the product. That is how you succeed and it's a philosophy you can go over and over.

In case you at this point have a powerful site with an enormous group it's really smart for you to pick a product that will intrigue that group.

Various Products

Remember too that you have the decision of selling lots of products. This is one more of the tremendous advantages of selling electronic product you can quickly add or take out things from your site without hoping to go through days forming and organizing.

There are potential gains and drawbacks to selling various products. Selling different products is wonderful if you have a significant site and you're using the fragile arrangement methodology (see the accompanying part).

This similarly allows you to offer an extent of expenses for different sorts of clients.

In light of everything focussing on everything will allow you to make more buzz and enthusiasm around that one express thing, and to make a more streamlined site that guides clients all to the buy page.

Picking Physical Products

Picking genuine product is barely extraordinary cooperation. Yet again the technique here should be to pick product that are material to your substance, and the standard peruser of your site.

All the while, they should moreover be products that are of extraordinary quality, and that fulfills a real need.

Luckily there is certainly not an undeniable clarification to make a significant frank theory and face a test by buying heaps of things in mass. You won't be looking at a situation where you have a stockroom stacked with whirly gigs. That suggests that you can seek after headings, and overall throw everything at the wall to see what sticks.

I truly recommend that you have an extent of different products at different sticker costs, to take exceptional consideration of every single kind of buyer.

However, also review that you make a commission on whatever is bought after the client visits Amazon. That suggests that the essential need should be to get the person to tap the association and to visit the page - perhaps more so than selling that specific product.

Get yourself a web have and make your site. Make one new page and spot the arrangements page copy you got there, close by your accomplice interface. You as of now have everything gotten up and positioned start selling and start making gains. We'll examine this resulting stage in the going with a segment.

Chapter 4

Developing a Market and Promoting the Products

The method for advancing by selling part things is to gather a horde of individuals first. This is the "secret" (to the degree that there is one), as it suggests that you need to truly contribute a couple of exertion and work to make the best arrangements.

The elevating news is that if you pick a point that you consider to be entrancing, you will fundamentally be getting a ton of money for achieving something you appreciate.

However, to show up as of now, you first need to create that group and gain their trust as an awe-inspiring phenomenon.

Are there substitute approaches to selling auxiliary products? Clearly we'll explore those in this part too. In any case, I still emphatically recommend that you develop that group and guarantee that people are enthusiastic about your picture.

Guidelines to Create a Brand That Sells

Gaining this kind of effect is troublesome. To arrive where people will buy things since you recommend them suggests money management a lot of energy and making a fair undertaking to offer certified benefits long term. These starting points by making a site close by significant solid areas for a media presence. Make an effort not to endeavor to sell right away, yet rather contribute energy fostering that trust and devotion through a mission of conveying incredible quality substance dependably.

The most compelling thing? Have a sensible, strong brand, with a mind-boggling mission statement, and a significant "buyer persona." (The buyer persona is the portrayal of your "ideal client.")

The best mistake to make is to endeavor to make an incredibly wide site with as extensive a charm as could be anticipated. Moreover, with the mechanized product you bought regardless, this can be a stirred-up method. The support behind that, can't avoid being that when you go extraordinarily sweeping, you similarly make a brand that is dull and bleak.

A "wellbeing" site for instance is unnecessarily nonexclusive and exorbitantly completed to death to be renowned. It infers matching the entire web. How might you hang out in such a submerged market?

Consider rather than having a site that is about Fitness for Over 40s. Then again shouldn't something be said about Paleo Fitness? Then again CrossFit. Then again Outdoor Fitness. Then again Hardcore Bodybuilding.

These decisions have a substantially more clear vested party, a significantly more clear mission statement, and a truly charming catch. They will each appeal to fewer people, yet people that the truth be told do address will far undoubtedly attract and be empowered that there is something out there expressly for them.

The brand should then be considered out of this undeniable and exciting objective. That suggests that when someone looks at your logo or your web synthesis, they should be aware instantly whether or not it will draw them. Your picture should immovably convey who it is for and what's the deal with it: and your substance should then back this up. The in front of your weight lifting site will likely be red and dim with heaps of faint pictures of solid areas for very, and articles about "supporting testosterone with compound lifts."

Meanwhile, the paleo wellbeing site will most likely be green and white with pictures of people running outer. From here, all your publicizing, all your social posts, and everything should be agreeable with this image.

What's more, thereafter, when you pick your branch-off thing, it should ideally address that indistinguishable group. Additionally, you will feature it like that, and sell it with that proposition.

What's also dire is that you give novel and new glad that shows real dominance. If you enroll a writer who has barely any understanding of the subject, then, at that point, you will never sell the accomplice thing. Why? Since all that could be done, is to investigate the subject and eject it in the most normal sounding manner for them.

That suggests that none of the substance will be new or sharp, and logic could be old or mistaken (because they will not have an idea about the guide by and large around alright toward perceiving when this is what is happening). You should think about yourself or find a writer who is truly energetic about the subject. Why? From that point forward they will have something new and stimulating to say. This is how you become a thought boss, and get people to tune in and to join: since they need another perspective. Be striking, Be novel, Be excited. Then at that point pick a thing that tends to the very same group. Do whatever it takes not to have energy for that. There are various decisions too which are recorded under.

Putting Your Link

As a branch-off publicist, selling couldn't be less complex. You're given one association, which is an association with advance a thing and you can then make arrangements and cash from wherever you place that association.

Most of us will put our association on a hello page/bargains page, but this is only a solitary decision. In this part, we'll look at how that capability, as well as a couple of extra decisions.

Making a Sales Page

An arrangements page is a page on a site that has been arranged expressly and completely goal of selling something. That suggests it won't give another substance (no articles) and conceivable the same associations or even adverts all the while. You don't want anything here that could gamble with redirecting people from the thing you're selling.

The arrangement of an arrangements page is routinely going to be very extended and tight, which will consequently encourage perusers to proceed to scroll and thus focus on the technique engaged with scrutinizing what you want to say. This makes it significantly harder for them to leave without buying, as they will feel like they consumed their time. By and large critical anyway is the arrangement. Make your endeavor to get it done precisely and you can take this delighted group and change them into restless buyers.

Persuasive creating is an exceptionally mind-boggling resource that can change you into a genius, these are not the robots you are looking for.

At last, in case you know how to use words to persuade a gathering, you will be evidently more effective at making bargains at getting people to become involved with your summary and all things considered at achieving any goal you're looking to. So how might you approach understanding this superpower. The following are a couple of clues that will help.

Grab thought

People are in a hurry and they would prefer not to peruse a great deal of text. On the off chance that you genuinely want to persuade your group first, you truly need to move them to examine what you want to say. How might you do this? One methodology is to open with serious areas of strength for A.

Another is to get through by using a story structure. The last choice capabilities honorably as we ordinarily find it genuinely testing to get some separation from a story without getting beyond what many would consider possible.

Appeal to measurable pieces of information

People aren't for the most part arranged to trust you taking everything into account they've never met you and they understand you want to propose to them. Maybe then let the numbers address you. The more figures you could articulate and the more experts you at any point can reference the more compelling your dispute will transform into.

Try to expect the concerns that your perusers will have and a while later fight them right away. For instance, you can determine how there are 'heaps of shocking-sounding proposals on the web yet point out that this isn't 'just another stunt.

Alleviate risk

People have regularly arranged to 'incident extreme aversion'. This suggests that they rush to grasp what they have than they are to secure a new thing. You truly need to take out any bet factor then, by offering unqualified commitments and free primers.

Specifically understand the proposition

This is the individual worth of your product how you are promising it can change your users lives. For example, if you are selling an eBook on health, you should observe that you're not selling an eBook on wellbeing.

What you're selling is the impression of having huge energy, torn abs, and bunches of assurance. You truly need to focus on that. Address the heart, and endeavor to get the peruser to feel something - ideally energy for buying your product.

Various high-level things will go with moment bargains pages like this, inferring that you can simply lift the substance rebate to use on your page.

With your arrangements page, you as of now essentially need to organize your group toward that page to start delivering changes. This ought to be conceivable through messages and by propelling your thing on your electronic diversion. You could recall adverts for the thing for the sidebar of your site and elsewhere.

Building a Store

If you are selling different auxiliary product (which is in like manner by and large great strategy), then, you can build a store to sell them from. That suggests that you'll highlight and propel things that are appropriate to your picture as you would do in an electronic business store. The vital certified differentiation is that when the buyer taps on your product, they will by and by rather be taken to an external page.

This is not difficult to do for example, you can do it by using the WordPress-obliging web business module called WooCommerce. This will allow you to make a store from your site where people can see your products. It maintains auxiliary substance, really proposing that expecting someone taps on a thing, they will be taken to the new page using your external reference.

More Ways to Sell

Anyway, shouldn't something be said about embedding joins inside the body of your articles? This is the sort of thing that not a lot of auxiliaries exploit anyway it's a remarkable strategy for adjusting a website or blog. Explain anything that subjects you're excited about covering and a while later install an accomplice interface into the message. You can propel the product unassumingly and anyone who is secured with your product could click it.

It looks like adding AdSense to your page, except you procure considerably more commission and you get to encourage people to tap the association. You could talk about reality with regards to the way that it acquires your cash.

The law in numerous locales of the planet is that you ought to deny that you are acquiring cash from those things. You can do this really by using a module that adds a message to the lower part of every single page on your site yet recall.

One of the most remarkable sorts of content for selling accomplice things is the vitally ten summaries. You can make a beginning article posting the best home rec focus gear if you're in the health business, or you can make an article sharing the most noteworthy workstations accessible expecting that you elucidate tech.

Whichever you do, this is great for delivering snaps and money, and will in like manner credit itself immaculately to rich pieces, which can really help your substance with hanging out in the SERPs (Search Engine Results Pages).

In this way, nothing is keeping you from putting an auxiliary association inside the body of an email. This is an extraordinary strategy for reaching people right inside their inbox when they may be available for your offers. Auxiliary associations can similarly go in eBooks. In case you are selling an electronic product or offering one for nothing, then, you can add interfaces with your PDF.

People examining this are presumably going to be particularly attracted to your picture and consequently inclined to buy what you recommend. These are qualified leads and that makes it the best spot to endeavor to sell a lot more noteworthy tickets.

Imagine selling a mechanized thing for $20 a pop, and a while later getting more money from each one people examining the book and regarding your direction.

Then again what might be said about putting an auxiliary association on a genuine flier or flyer? The best method for using this is to use a more critical and clear URL and subsequently have it redirect to your auxiliary association. That way you can truly elevate your thing up close and personal.

The spot of these thoughts is mostly to display that you don't really for each situation should be successfully selling the thing: you can endeavor the fragile sell by basically adding the association, perhaps with an image. This capability is commendable for real things (especially if you use a particularly arranged button and the thing is successfully associated with the product on the page). If you have a notable site with a lot of watchers and a lot of content, then, at that point, fundamentally twisting around buy participates all through as such can provoke lots of arrangements gushing in and they all add up.

There are much more ways you can use accomplice goes along with, you just should be innovative. Assessment and endeavor different things and you might be surprised what ends up being savage for yourself as well as your product.

PPC Advertising and Other Marketing

Nevertheless, envision a situation in which you don't have a horde of individuals. Envision a situation where you're not an awe-inspiring phenomenon who has obtained the trust of your perusers.

For this present circumstance, you ought to find approaches to sending visitors to your arrangements page.

Luckily you can do this actually through PPC (Pay Per Click) stages like Facebook and AdWords.

PPC infers that you potentially pay when someone truly taps on your advert. You close what your most noteworthy spend "per click" will be, and what the restriction of your monetary arrangement will be as well. In case you set your per click to spend too low, your advancement won't show when there are heaps of battling notices from various brands in a comparable forte. Set it unreasonably high, and you presumably won't bring in cash.

While putting notices on Facebook, you will need to target what their personality is shown to considering information that clients share with the social site. Those include:

Age

Sex

Region

Recreation exercises and interests

Work title

Level of pay

Interests of others And more.

While putting commercials on Google through AdWords, the point is to ponder not simply the interests of the person (considering what they are searching for - the "watchwords") yet furthermore the motivation behind that person.

The plan is a critical idea for PPC, considering the way that it tells you whether someone is investigating, or wanting to buy.

If they are investigating, they could search for "best PC games this year." If they are expecting to buy, then, at that point, they could glance through the name of the PC game, or "humble PC games." You can moreover use "negative watchwords" to block expresses that could suggest someone isn't enthused about buying consequently has some unsuitable reason, (for instance, "free download"). The mark of PPC is to ensure that people only snap the association accepting they are most likely going to buy from you. This cuts down the aggregate you spend, while growing the reasonable advantage. That suggests the adverts ought to be as immovably "centered around" to the best person as could truly be anticipated, even with the final product of driving off people who will not in all likelihood need to buy using the right text. The association should clearly direct people to an arrangements page to extend your advantages. You then, need to focus in on the change speed of your site. Accordingly, if your show page is exquisitely created it could change more than 1% of visitors (meaning 1% of visitors buy from you). The higher you get this number, the more you can bear spending on your advancing while at this point obtaining an advantage.

Direct Selling Through Facebook and Other Platforms

You moreover have the decision to sell directly through those various stages. Nothing still needs to be stopped you from sharing an auxiliary interface with your Facebook pack, or to your Instagram (in your profile, or when you can incorporate the swipe-up feature stories). This is a significant strategy for building an associated swarm if you don't have the secret sauce or time to make a site.

Chapter 5

Powerful Modern Tools and Strategies

Selling a blend of various items - including computerized, administrations and physical is undeniably more remarkable because it consolidates the sorts of huge deals you can make by building a dedicated crowd with the volume that comes from moving bunches of actual items. What's more, here's another thing to remember: having such a different arrangement of subsidiary items to sell on your site implies that you have the choice to add things that are "fantasy" deals. A model? I once sold an MBA through an associate connection. This was through EDx, which is a possibly enormously productive subsidiary program, however additionally an illustration of one that you should pursue.

The test Overseeing and shuffling those various things! To this end, the enormous, serious brands will utilize apparatuses that smooth out this interaction, and that give them admittance to the absolute most rewarding offshoot programs on the web.

Significant Tools for Taking Affiliate Marketing to the Next Level

One of these instruments is Genius Link. Through Genius (https://www.geni.us/), you can append numerous various records and afterward add their offshoot programs. This functions admirably with Amazon, as it permits you to add accounts with every one of the different nearby forms of Amazon.

Each connection will then, at that point, send the client to the right rendition of Amazon in view of their area, meaning you don't have to stress over losing clients! You can likewise add various different projects in any case, like Barnes&Noble, BestBuy, and iTunes.

From here, you can create a connection from Amazon as effectively as getting the URL to the business page, and afterward gluing it into a container. Assuming you have the Chrome module, you can simply click that button not too far off when your program is pointed at the page.

A comparative choice is something many refer to as Trackonomics (https://www.trackonomics.net). This device works likewise, however allows you to add things from a FAR bigger rundown of subsidiaries. That incorporates any semblance of the previously mentioned EDx. Even better, Trackonomics can allow you to look for items in a huge swath of various subsidiary records, and afterward utilize the choice that makes the most money.

All in all, assuming you are selling a cell phone, you can now look at the commission on that cell phone were you to sell it from Amazon, versus the commission were you to sell it direct from the maker. Versus Best Buy, versus each and every choice out there. The two devices likewise let you track snaps and buys, to distinguish which of your connections is the most well known, to recognize when a connection is down, or to perceive the amount you have procured in a given time span.

More Tools

These devices will assist you with taking your partner's profit to another level, however, there are a lot more choices out there too for those that need to make a more smoothed-out plan of action and pipe. For example, it is practically vital to use Google Analytics to follow the outcome of your site and individual pages. You can perceive how you rank for various terms, advance those terms, and afterward perceive how those pages are prompting the business page, and which courses procure the most commission.
Utilizing instruments that let you lead A/B tests on your presentation page can likewise assist you with further developing it to the point that it greatly increments transformations.

In Conclusion

In this manner, that is all that you need to know to build a significantly successful auxiliary displaying business.

Whether you save things clearly or pull out all the stops relies upon you, but I excitedly recommend you notice the direction in this book and make a pass at selling veritable things that have wide charm and gigantic expenses as well as the standard mechanized eBooks and courses.

The model cycle for selling auxiliary product is fundamental.

Find progressed things and get an accomplice interface.

Make an arrangements page.

Put interface on bargains page.

Send traffic to the bargains page both from your site and through exhibit. Stop responding until the product stop selling then rehash this interaction. I'm recommending that you fairly change this model to get extra money and create a more grounded, long stretch strategy.

Here is the new strategy

Make a site and develop a horde of individuals that trusts in you and value what you do. Do this by making truly unique and lively substance with a strong visual brand and mission statement. Find several costly auxiliary things and organizations and make bargains pages for those, then "ship off" them from your site by using email effects and secrets to make the exposure. Find the things that are ideal and a short time later send more visitors here through paid publicizing. In the meantime, sell various unobtrusive high-level products, Amazon genuine products and organizations through articles and destinations that makes you advance using SEO. Anything which you do you can see the value in acquiring cash while you rest and the more you dissect the more useful your business technique will transform into.

www.ingramcontent.com/pod-product-compliance
Lightning Source LLC
Chambersburg PA
CBHW050319220526
45465CB00005B/2052